IF SAVED

Dr. Johnny Woodard~DD

For more information about the Bread Of Life International Bible Correspondence Institute, we can be contacted at the information given below.

The Bread Of Life International
Bible Correspondence Institute
P.O. Box 334
Kirbyville, Texas
75956

bolbcs@gmail.com

http://www.simplesite.com/

Foreword

The doctrine of eternal security or "Once Saved, Always Saved" is one of the most debated and controversial issues in the churches today. I have discussed that issue on many occasions and preached many messages on it through my over 40 years in the ministry. I have some dear missionary friends that work with the North American Indians that came up with the phrase, "If Saved, Always Saved," which makes a lot more sense to me. Many of those who disagree with the eternal security of the believer think that it gives a child of God the license to just live it up and sin all you want to and still die and go to Heaven, regardless of how they lived their lives after becoming a child of God.

This study on Eternal Security will show the fallacy of that kind of teaching and expose the truth concerning the difference between relationship and fellowship. I myself had some problems understanding the teaching of eternal security when I first entered the ministry in 1979. We will examine closely the scriptures that teach the truths of eternal security and also look at others that seem to contradict it in this book.

All scripture references used are from the King James Bible. My prayer is that this study will help you to understand the eternal security of the believer and will motivate us to do more to advance the cause of Christ.

Dr. Johnny Woodard~DD
President:
The Bread Of Life International
Bible Correspondence Institute

Table Of Contents

Chapter 1
How Can These Things Be?.. 1

Chapter 2
Set Free Or On Probation? 7

Chapter 3
Rewriting God's Word 15

Chapter 4
What God's Word Doesn't Say 19

Chapter 5
Not What But Who 29

Chapter 6
Why Not Just Live It Up? 33

Chapter 7
In Conclusion 39

Other Books Available 41

Chapter I
How Can These Things Be?

John 3:9 Nicodemus answered and said unto him, How can these things be?

One of the biggest obstacles Satan uses to deny the eternal security of the believer is to confuse people about the difference between relationship and fellowship. I have four children, 3 daughters and one son. There is no crime or evil deed they can do that will result in any one of them going back in time and not being born to me and my wife Jewel.

Heb 7:25 Wherefore he is able also to save them to the uttermost that come unto God by him, seeing he ever liveth to make intercession for them.

The writer of Hebrews used the word "uttermost" in describing those who Jesus saves. The word uttermost carries the meaning of being entirely full or complete. When a lost sinner comes to Jesus and trusts Him for salvation, a marvelous thing takes place. He or she is born into God's family and all their sins from past, present to future are covered by the blood of Jesus. For to be truly saved and then lose salvation or become unsaved, the meaning of uttermost could not be applied to the finished work of redemption Jesus accomplished on the cross.

John 3:1-3
1 There was a man of the Pharisees, named Nicodemus, a ruler of the Jews:
2 The same came to Jesus by night, and said unto him, Rabbi, we know that thou art a teacher come from God: for no man can do these miracles that thou doest, except God be with him.
3 Jesus answered and said unto him, Verily, verily, I say unto thee, Except a man be born again, he cannot see the kingdom of God.
4 Nicodemus saith unto him, How can a man be born when he is old? can he enter the second time into his mother's womb, and be born?

There are many Bible truths to be gained from Jesus' encounter with Nicodemus one night many years ago. Nicodemus was a very educated man, a Pharisee and a member of the Sanhedrin Council. The Sanhedrin men were members of the Pharisees who acted as judges in matters of the Jewish laws and customs.

Nicodemus came to Jesus at night mainly by fear of what would happen to him if he were seen in a conversation with Jesus. However, Nicodemus believed that Jesus was sent by God and wanted to know more about His teaching. The miracles Jesus performed made a great impression on him and convinced him that he needed to know all he could about Him and His ministry. When Jesus told him that he needed to be born again, he could not understand how anyone could be born twice. What he did not understand is that Jesus was not referring to physical births, but to Spiritual births. Jesus later on explained to Nicodemus about the true meaning of being born again.

When a person is born again into God's family by faith in Jesus Christ, God does not change one as most think a change is, they become a new creature. I have used an illustration of melting down an old Studebaker and taking the metal from it and making a shiny new Cadillac. In order for that Studebaker to become a Cadillac the old Studebaker has to be completely destroyed and all the impurities removed and poured into a new mold that transforms it into an entirely different vehicle that is brand new.

2 Corinthians 5:17 Therefore if any man be in Christ, he is a new creature: old things are passed away; behold, all things are become new.

Romans 6:6 Knowing this, that our old man is crucified with him, that the body of sin might be destroyed, that henceforth we should not serve sin.

One must also understand that by taking Cadillac emblems and putting them on a Studebaker doesn't make it a Cadillac. Putting on good works doesn't make a person a child of God any more than changing emblems and stickers on a vehicle. By far many church members do not understand what takes place at the salvation experience. One's body is not saved at that instance because all will continue to grow older or die unexpectedly. The point is that our bodies will not be saved until Jesus returns back to earth and gives all of God's children a glorified body.

Philippians 3:21 Who shall change our vile body, that it may be fashioned like unto his glorious body, according to the working whereby he is able even to subdue all things unto himself.

We also need to remember that after Jesus died on the cross He was never again approached by Satan or any of his followers. The reason for that is that when He died on the cross He paid the sin debt for all mankind and had completely defeated all of Satan's attacks on Him to try and get Him to sin and fail doing what God sent Him to do. Everyone needs to understand that Jesus paid the sin debt for all mankind's sins from Adam until all those living when He returns to earth to reign for all eternity.

1 John 2:1-3
1 My little children, these things write I unto you, that ye sin not. And if any man sin, we have an advocate with the Father, Jesus Christ the righteous:
2 And he is the propitiation for our sins: and not for ours only, but also for the sins of the whole world.

G2434 *hilasmos*
atonement, i.e. (concretely) an expiator:--propitiation.

The word propitiation carries the thought of atonement. Jesus death was the final atonement for all sins committed that separated man from a Holy God.

Romans 5:9-11
9 Much more then, being now justified by his blood, we shall be saved from wrath through him.
10 For if, when we were enemies, we were reconciled to God by the death of his Son, much more, being reconciled, we shall be saved by his life.
11 And not only so, but we also joy in God through our Lord Jesus Christ, by whom we have now received the atonement.

The Old Testament tells us of the many different kinds of sacrifices required to keep one in the right standing with a Holy God. When we get to the New Testament and read where the veil in the temple was rent in twain from top to bottom we know that the final sacrifice for sins had been made.

Hebrews 10:12 But this man, after he had offered one sacrifice for sins for ever, sat down on the right hand of God;

The One that the writer of the letter to the Hebrews is referring to is none other than Jesus Himself. Note the words forever. Jesus died one time for all the sins of mankind.

As it is impossible for a human to go back in time and be unborn, so it is with those who are born again, they cannot go back in time when they were born again and be unborn Spiritually.

Chapter II
Set Free Or On Probation?

John 8:36 If the Son therefore shall make you free, ye shall be free indeed.

We know that the wages of sin is death and also know that a Holy God does not allow sin to enter into His presence. While Jesus was dying on the cross He cried out to God and asked Him why did He forsake Him?

Matthew 27:46 And about the ninth hour Jesus cried with a loud voice, saying, Eli, Eli, lama sabachthani? that is to say, My God, my God, why hast thou forsaken me?

The answer for Jesus' question is simple, the sins of the entire human race was placed upon Jesus and God turned His face away at that instant.

John 1:29 The next day John seeth Jesus coming unto him, and saith, Behold the Lamb of God, which taketh away the sin of the world.

Since we know that Jesus died for the sins of all mankind, how does that relate to a believer's relationship with a Holy God who does not allow sin to come into His presence? There are several different scriptures that answer that question.

Psalms 103:12 *As far as the east is from the west,* **so** *far hath he removed our transgressions from us.*

The Psalmist stated that God removes one's sins as far as the east is from the west, which simply means it is unending.

1 John 2:2 *And he is the propitiation for our sins: and not for ours only, but also for* **the sins of** *the whole world.*

The word propitiation literally means atonement. From the very beginning God had required man to offer up sacrifices as an atonement for transgressions against Him prior to the death of Jesus. The Old Testament describes five basic types of sacrifices to be offered up as an atonement for sins committed. They were as follows.

  The Burnt Offering (Leviticus 1)
  The Meat Offering (Leviticus 2)
  The Peace Offering (Leviticus 3)
  The Sin Offering (Leviticus 4)
  The Trespass Offering (Leviticus 5)

Romans 3:20 *Therefore by the deeds of the law there shall no flesh be justified in his sight: for by the law is the knowledge of sin.*

Sadly there are many different religions today that are still teaching that living a moral life will get you to Heaven. When the veil in the Temple was rent in twain from top to bottom, the time for Old Testament sacrifices came to an end. No more would there be a need for the High Priest to enter into the Holy Of Holies and make a sacrifice for the sins of the people.

Hebrews 10:26 For if we sin wilfully after that we have received the knowledge of the truth, there remaineth no more sacrifice for sins,

The writer of the Book Of Hebrews gave a chilling warning to those who would continue making sacrifices after Jesus offered up His life as the final sacrifice for the sins of all mankind. In 70 A.D. the Roman armies led by General Titus torched the Temple and burnt it to the ground. A Bible prophecy that Jesus made before His death was fulfilled at that time.

Matthew 24:1-2
1 And Jesus went out, and departed from the temple: and his disciples came to him for to shew him the buildings of the temple.
2 And Jesus said unto them, See ye not all these things? verily I say unto you, There shall not be left here one stone upon another, that shall not be thrown down.

I firmly believe that God's Children should live lives that honor the great sacrifice Jesus made for us all, but under no circumstances does Godly living earn a person a place in Heaven. Don't ever forget the words that the Old Testament prophet Isaiah spoke many years ago to a rebellious people that had drifted far from God's will for their lives.

Isaiah 64:6 But we are all as an unclean* thing, *and all our righteousnesses* are *as filthy rags; and we all do fade as a leaf; and our iniquities, like the wind, have taken us away.

My illustration of what our righteousness looks like in the eyes of a Holy God is as follows:

Suppose a person died of leprosy, which is a terrible and painful disease that afflicts one's body with open running sores. Suppose that person wore those same clothes day after day until he died. Taking those disease-ridden clothes and putting them on is what our good deeds look like to a Holy God who demands perfection.

I remember as a young boy hearing about the death of Hank Williams on January 1, 1953. To me he was the greatest country music singer ever and also wrote many great Gospel Songs. Hank started singing in church with his mother and later on rose to fame and fortune having hit after hit in his career. One of his most popular gospel songs is "I Saw The Light." Being a part of my family's Bluegrass Gospel singing group for many years, we sang that song many times. There is another popular Gospel Hymn that carries the same tune as I Saw The Light. Look at the message in that great old Gospel Hymn.

He Set Me Free

Once like a bird in prison I dwelt,
No freedom from my sorrow I felt.
But Jesus came and listened to me,
And glory to God, He set me free.

Chorus:
He set me free, yes He set me free,
And He broke the bonds of prison for me.
I'm glory bond my Jesus to see,
For glory to God, He set me free.

Now I am climbing higher each day,
Darkness of night has drifted away.
My feet are planted on higher ground,
And glory to God, I'm homeward bound.

Repeat Chorus

Goodbye to sin and things that confound,
Not of this world shall turn me around.
Daily I'm working, I'm praying too,
And glory to God, I'm going through.

Repeat Chorus

John 8:36 If the Son therefore shall make you free, ye shall be free indeed.

We have to understand what a believer is freed from concerning the sins that would prevent us from being a part of God's family. We have already showed that Jesus died for the sins of the whole world, so how are we set free from our sins?

Consider four important facts concerning the sins that separate mankind from God.

1. We are not set free from the presence of sin, it is rampant everywhere. There is no escaping its presence in so many areas of our world.

2. We are not set free from the influence of sin. We are under attack everyday by Satan's army of evil spirits out to entice us to sin, thus causing pain and grief to our Blessed Saviour, Jesus Christ.

3. We are not set free from the consequences of sin. Everyday of our life we are getting closer to our death and leaving this sin ridden world. All manner of sickness and acts of evil are a direct result of sin.

4. Lastly, we are only saved from the penalty of sin. The wages of sin is death The Apostle Paul wrote in his letter to the Roman believers. Thank God there is more to that scripture that tells us that the gift of God is eternal life.

Romans 6:23 For the wages of sin is death; but the gift of God is eternal life through Jesus Christ our Lord.

Note that God's gift to all believers is eternal life. To be saved and then be unsaved would have to contradict Paul's writing, as we will see in other scriptures later on. Jesus paid our sin debt once and for all.

Chapter III
Rewriting God's Word

John 7:38-39
38 He that believeth on me, as the scripture hath said, out of his belly shall flow rivers of living water.
39 (But this spake he of the Spirit, which they that believe on him should receive: for the Holy Ghost was not yet given; because that Jesus was not yet glorified.)

On more than one occasion The Apostle Paul wrote to the churches warning them of another Gospel and another Jesus being preached. Satan has been a master at perverting God's Word since Adam and Eve were deceived in The Garden Of Eden. In this chapter we will see how he has deceived multitudes into changing the meaning of what God's Word teaches.

Suppose a saved person could lose salvation, what would it mean?

One would have to:

1. Declare God's Grace to be insufficient.

You would have to believe that the grace of God is insufficient to save you. It is by God's grace we are saved. To say you could lose salvation would mean that God's grace for you to be saved is not sufficient to accomplish its purpose.

Ephesians 2:8 For by grace are ye saved through faith; and that not of yourselves: it is the gift of God:

2. Get Christ to take back His righteousness.

Because of when Christ died on the cross at Calvary, it is His righteousness that enables us to stand justified before a Holy God. To lose salvation would mean that Jesus would remove His righteousness from us.

2 Corinthians 5: 21 For he hath made him **to be** *sin for us, who knew no sin; that we might be made the righteousness of God in him.*

3. Break the seal of The Holy Spirit

God the Father sealed us by the Holy Spirit until the day of redemption. For us to lose salvation God The Father would have to break the seal of the Holy Spirit and He would no longer be dwelling in us. The day of redemption refers to the redemption of our physical bodies that will be changed into a glorified body when Jesus returns back to earth.

Ephesians 4:30 And grieve not the holy Spirit of God, whereby ye are sealed unto the day of redemption.

Break the seal of the Holy Spirit.

Romans 6:22-23
22 But now being made free from sin, and become servants to God, ye have your fruit unto holiness, and

4. Change the meaning of "Everlasting and Eternal".
　We would have to change the meaning of both everlasting and eternal to mean something different than it does.

Romans 6:22-23
22 But now being made free from sin, and become servants to God, ye have your fruit unto holiness, and the end everlasting life.
23 For the wages of sin is death; but the gift of God is eternal life through Jesus Christ our Lord.

5. To lose salvation would be to mutilate the body of Christ.
　For a person that was saved to be lost, part of the Body of Christ would be amputated. When Christ presents His Bride to the Father, it will be a perfect Bride, without blemish or spot, not a mutilated corpse.

1 Corinthians 12:12-13
12 For as the body is one, and hath many members, and all the members of that one body, being many, are one body: so also is Christ.
13 For by one Spirit are we all baptized into one body,

whether we be Jews or Gentiles, whether we be bond or free; and have been all made to drink into one Spirit.

6. Define the meaning of the most quoted New Testament Scripture in the Bible John 3:16.

John 3:16 For God so loved the world, that he gave his only begotten Son, that whosoever believeth in him should not perish, but have everlasting life.

The greatest gift one could ever possibly receive is the gift of eternal life. People may win the lottery and become an instant millionaire or receive a huge inheritance. They can have all the things this world can provide except eternal life. I have heard that you will never see a Hearse pulling a U-Haul trailer behind it. Another person asked someone concerning a departed rich person how much did they leave behind. They replied stating that they left it all. Satan is a master at perverting God's Word. Don't be deceived into believing that God is going to take back the greatest gift of all, eternal life through Jesus Christ Our Lord.

Chapter IV
What The Word Doesn't Say

There are a few scriptures that some take out of context to teach that a person can lose salvation. We will look at some of them and show how they interpret them.

Matthew 7:21-23
21 Not every one that saith unto me, Lord, Lord, shall enter into the kingdom of heaven; but he that doeth the will of my Father which is in heaven.
22 Many will say to me in that day, Lord, Lord, have we not prophesied in thy name? and in thy name have cast out devils? and in thy name done many wonderful works?
23 And then will I profess unto them, I never knew you: depart from me, ye that work iniquity.

It is absurd to teach that the above scriptures refer in any way to a person losing salvation. One needs to consider the context of why Jesus said what He did. The preceding verses states that He was referring to false prophets, not believers. In verse 23 Jesus made it clear that those who were calling Him Lord were never Christians at all because He never knew them in a personal relationship and their lives proved that they were not true children of God.

Matthew 24:13 But he that shall endure unto the end, the same shall be saved.

To teach that the above scripture refers to losing salvation by not enduring until the end of the great tribulation would be teaching a works salvation and not saved by God's grace. No one is saved by enduring any kind of trial, it is the grace of God that saves all.

Titus 2:11 For the grace of God that bringeth salvation hath appeared to all men,

1 Corinthians 9:27 But I keep under my body, and bring it into subjection: lest that by any means, when I have preached to others, I myself should be a castaway.

Paul is not referring to losing salvation but rather to losing his Christian testimony and influence over a carnal minded bunch of people. The word castaway is used only one time in the entire Bible and it refers to one being rejected or worthless. Compare the false teaching of losing salvation with the words of Jesus concerning being cast out or rejected.

John 6:37 All that the Father giveth me shall come to me; and him that cometh to me I will in no wise cast out.

Sadly, many people are trusting in trying to earn salvation by doing good works and as a result think that to not please God by living Godly lifestyles they will be rejected and removed from God's family. Rest assured, once a person puts their trust in Jesus alone they are safe and kept secure for all eternity.

Galatians 5:4 Christ is become of no effect unto you, whosoever of you are justified by the law; ye are fallen from grace.

Some scriptures in Paul's letter to the Galatians are some of the favorites used to try and prove that salvation can be lost. What they don't teach is that the main purpose why Paul wrote the letter is to correct the false teaching that keeping the Mosaic Law and the Old Testament practice of circumcision was necessary for one to be saved. He had strong words condemning that false teaching.

Galatians 1:6-9
6 I marvel that ye are so soon removed from him that called you into the grace of Christ unto another gospel:
7 Which is not another; but there be some that trouble you, and would pervert the gospel of Christ.
8 But though we, or an angel from heaven, preach any other gospel unto you than that which we have preached unto you, let him be accursed.
9 As we said before, so say I now again, If any man preach any other gospel unto you than that ye have received, let him be accursed.

The another Jesus and another gospel Paul was referring to was what I stated above concerning keeping Old Testament practices, which were done away with as necessary for salvation when Jesus died for our sins.

Romans 3:28 Therefore we conclude that a man is justified by faith without the deeds of the law.

When Paul used the phrase fallen from grace, he was referring to those being deceived into believing they could not be saved by God's grace alone and had departed from his teaching of salvation by grace alone.

Revelation 2:7 He that hath an ear, let him hear what the Spirit saith unto the churches; To him that overcometh will I give to eat of the tree of life, which is in the midst of the paradise of God.

We read what Jesus revealed to The Apostle John concerning the Spiritual condition of the seven churches in Asia Minor. The first church He dealt with was the church at Ephesus. The church there had a lot of good things going for it but had become cold and indifferent when people wanted to come into the fellowship. It was because of the problems of their stand against false Apostles that had caused problems in the church (vs. 2&3).

We need to understand what it means to be an overcomer. Since God's standard is sinless perfection, who can ever live up to His standards? One verse in simple words defines who a true overcomer is.

1 John 5:5 Who is he that overcometh the world, but he that believeth that Jesus is the Son of God?

Can anyone say with a truthful heart that his or her lifestyle is sinless?

1 John 1:10 If we say that we have not sinned, we make him a liar, and his word is not in us.

All need to serve God out of love for Him giving His Only Begotten Son to die in our place for our sins so we can have eternal life. We are true overcomers because of our faith in Jesus alone for all hopes of spending eternity with Him in Heaven.

2 Peter 2:19-22
19 While they promise them liberty, they themselves are the servants of corruption: for of whom a man is overcome, of the same is he brought in bondage.
20 For if after they have escaped the pollutions of the world through the knowledge of the Lord and Saviour Jesus Christ, they are again entangled therein, and overcome, the latter end is worse with them than the beginning.
21 For it had been better for them not to have known the way of righteousness, than, after they have known it, to turn from the holy commandment delivered unto them.
22 But it is happened unto them according to the true proverb, The dog is turned to his own vomit again; and the sow that was washed to her wallowing in the mire.

More of the favorite scriptures used to try and teach that a saved person can be lost. Before going any further we have to understand who the "they" are that Peter was referring to. The entire chapter is referring to false prophets and teachers, not true believers.

2 Peter 2:1 But there were false prophets also among the people, even as there shall be false teachers among you, who privily shall bring in damnable heresies, even denying the Lord that bought them, and bring upon themselves swift destruction.

When keeping that thought in mind it is easy to see that Peter was referring to unsaved people that were deceiving many by their false teaching. Peter simply states that it would have been better for them not to have known the truth than to know it and turn from it. When we see what they were teaching and their wicked lifestyles it is evident that they were not true believers as some want to teach. When we think about the dog returning to his vomit and the sow to her wallow, a scripture Paul wrote to a carnal minded church in Corinth, Greece comes to mind.

2 Corinthians 5:17 Therefore if any man be in Christ, he is a new creature: old things are passed away; behold, all things are become new.

Why did Paul use the word creature instead of man or woman or boy or girl concerning the salvation experience? Simple: it is because Jesus referred to His true followers as sheep. Had Peter been referring to true believers, they would have been changed from a dog or a sow into a sheep. By stating that they never had a life changing experience, we know that Peter was not referring to a child of God losing salvation, but rather to unsaved false prophets that were deceiving many of God's children.

Hebrews 6:1-6
1 Therefore leaving the principles of the doctrine of Christ, let us go on unto perfection; not laying again the foundation of repentance from dead works, and of faith toward God,
2 Of the doctrine of baptisms, and of laying on of hands, and of resurrection of the dead, and of eternal judgment.
3 And this will we do, if God permit.
4 For it is impossible for those who were once enlightened, and have tasted of the heavenly gift, and were made partakers of the Holy Ghost,
5 And have tasted the good word of God, and the powers of the world to come,
6 If they shall fall away, to renew them again unto repentance; seeing they crucify to themselves the Son of God afresh, and put him to an open shame.

Some of the most troubling scriptures a child of God has dealing with eternal security is in Hebrews Chapter 6. I will admit that when I first entered the ministry over 40 years ago I had trouble understanding these scriptures. The writer of this letter or book as we refer to it is not identified. Most all Bible Scholars believe that it was written by The Apostle

Paul, who was a high-ranking member of the Pharisees and well educated in the Jewish laws. From the very beginning the Jewish leaders were against Jesus and His teachings. It was them who had Jesus betrayed and ultimately sentenced to death because of treason by Pontius Pilate.

Keeping that in mind, we know that the Jewish leaders did not believe that a person could be saved by faith in Jesus alone. In fact they didn't even believe He was God's son and their Messiah. When we get to chapter 6 the writer states it is time to move on from the principles or teachings concerning Christ but driving home the point that in order for a child of God to be saved and then lost and then saved again Jesus would have to come to earth, live a sinless life and die for mankind's sins again in order to be saved again.

The key word to understanding the message of this text is "tasted". Tasting of any substance, whether it is food, drink, medicine or any other substance that was essential for the body was of no use unless it is consumed and not rejected or spit out. One cannot survive without food or water indefinitely. A starving person can be at death's door and have all the food needed to save his or her life and not put the food into their mouth. It is of no value to them if they taste it and then spit it out.

Jesus used a similar illustration concerning one of the seven churches in Asia Minor in the Book Of Revelation.

Revelation 3:14-16
14 And unto the angel of the church of the Laodiceans write; These things saith the Amen, the faithful and true witness, the beginning of the creation of God;

15 I know thy works, that thou art neither cold nor hot: I would thou wert cold or hot.
16 So then because thou art lukewarm, and neither cold nor hot, I will spue thee out of my mouth.

When we think about how the Jewish leaders knew about the teachings of Jesus and how the Old Testament scriptures foretold His coming, instead of embracing Him as their Messiah, they rejected Him in the same way that Jesus rejected the actions and beliefs of the Laodicean Church previously mentioned. Taking those facts into consideration, like those referred to by the scriptures in Hebrews Chapter 6, it is not referring to believers but unsaved Jewish leaders who rejected Jesus as the God Sent Messiah who He was.

Chapter V
Not What But Who

Romans 8:35 Who shall separate us from the love of Christ? shall tribulation, or distress, or persecution, or famine, or nakedness, or peril, or sword?

Paul asks a question to the Roman believers, and then answers the question himself.

I have been told by some of those who don't believe in the security of the believer that although circumstances cannot separate a person from Christ, a person can separate himself.

*Note: (35) Paul's question asked **who**, not what could separate one from the love of Christ.*

The early church was a persecuted church. Keep in mind that families were torn apart and many were persecuted unto death. He made it very plain first of all that even though families were torn apart, fellow believers were separated and even put to death, no one could separate them from God's love.

(35) Who: Paul is saying that no matter if a person goes through tribulation, distress, persecution, famine, nakedness

or peril, the person will not be separated from God by those circumstances. Tribulation, distress, persecution, famine, nakedness or peril are not <u>persons,</u> they are <u>events in a person's life.</u> These things might lead to a child of God losing his life here on earth, but his salvation remains secure.

(38) Paul went further on to enter the Spiritual realm and to state that even death, angels, principalities, powers, nor things present, or things to come, can separate a child of God from His love. Events in one's life could not separate one from God's love, death could not separate one from God's love, nor could satanic powers.

Principalities and powers refer to satanic forces that attack God's children constantly. He ends here by reassuring them that nothing they are facing in the present nor anything they face in the future will separate them from God's love.

(39) Height or depth.
- a. Height refers to any circumstance a person might arise to. A person might gain great worldly prestige and honor and turn from God, this great prestige cannot separate him from God. God will not disown him.

- b. Depth refers to one who might fall to the lowest ranks of humanity. He can fall to the lowest circumstances, rags to riches, become a drunken bum, and yet still be secure in his relationship with God.

Many people cannot separate relationship with God from fellowship with God.

To sum it up, Paul's answer to his own question was in response to the believers at Rome that were being influenced by the Jews who did not accept the doctrine of salvation by grace alone. His reply was simple. No one or nobody can separate a child of God from Him.

We read in Peter's letter to believers that salvation was secure no matter how bad their circumstances were.

1 Peter 1: 3-5
13 Blessed be the God and Father of our Lord Jesus Christ, which according to his abundant mercy hath begotten us again unto a lively hope by the resurrection of Jesus Christ from the dead,
4 To an inheritance incorruptible, and undefiled, and that fadeth not away, reserved in heaven for you,
5 Who are kept by the power of God through faith unto salvation ready to be revealed in the last time.

This is a letter written to the early believers who were undergoing tremendous persecution.

(vs. 3) Peter first tells them that even though they face persecution and death, they had a hope that was alive and well. Hope, because Jesus Christ was alive and had risen from the grave.

(vs. 4) Because of His victory over death and the grave, they had an inheritance awaiting them.

Note what he said about this inheritance:

a. **It is incorruptible.** It could not start out as something good and then be corrupted into something bad.

b. **It is undefiled.** It is not something that started out as pure and then became contaminated by sin.

c. **Fadeth not away.** Referring to a light that fades into darkness. Heaven is a place of eternal light and Hell is a place of eternal darkness. Their inheritance won't start out as light and fade away into darkness.

d. **Reserved in Heaven for you.**

e. Reserved: To guard from loss by keeping an eye on the reservation made. What Peter is saying is that a place is reserved in Heaven for them by God Himself and God Himself is keeping an eye on it, so it won't be lost.

(vs. 5) This verse tells them why their inheritance is secure; it is kept by the power of God Himself.

a. God cannot be corrupted

b. God cannot be defiled

c. God's light and glory never fades away.

d. No power anywhere is greater than God's power and can take our inheritance away from Him.

So, all who are saved by the blood of Jesus, have a home awaiting them in Heaven, that will be there awaiting them, no matter what.

Chapter VI
Why Not Just Live It Up?

I have heard it over and over "You ole Baptists think you can do anything you want to and then die and go to Heaven." I am a Baptist and do believe that a true child of God can do whatever he wants to and die and go to Heaven. The whole key to that belief is based on what a true child of God wants to do.

The Apostle Paul was the greatest missionary who ever lived except Jesus Christ Who left Heaven to come to earth to redeem fallen man. Read how he described his walk with Christ in Romans 7.

Romans 7:14-21
14 For we know that the law is spiritual: but I am carnal, sold under sin.
15 For that which I do I allow not: for what I would, that do I not; but what I hate, that do I.
16 If then I do that which I would not, I consent unto the law that it is good.
17 Now then it is no more I that do it, but sin that dwelleth in me.
18 For I know that in me (that is, in my flesh,) dwelleth no good thing: for to will is present with me; but how to

perform that which is good I find not.
19 For the good that I would I do not: but the evil which I would not, that I do.
20 Now if I do that I would not, it is no more I that do it, but sin that dwelleth in me.
21 I find then a law, that, when I would do good, evil is present with me.

Paul told of his struggles about overcoming Satan's attacks, which were many, to say the least. He made it clear that he did not always do what he should do and that at times he also did things that he shouldn't do. The key to these verses I found in verse 18.

18 For I know that in me (that is, in my flesh,) dwelleth no good thing: for <u>to will is present with me</u>; but how to perform that which is good I find not.

The difference between a true child of God and an unbeliever is that all of God's children are indwelled by The Holy Spirit. The Holy Spirit always leads those He dwells in to only do things that are pleasing to God and also to not do things that are displeasing to Him. It is defined as either grieving the Holy Spirit or quenching the Holy Spirit.

I was saved at the very young age of 7 years but was not raised in a Christian home. I never was involved in horrible crimes or was addicted to drugs or alcohol, etc. I however did not live a Godly life after being faithful to Church and living for the Lord the best I knew how. I recall riding a bicycle 7 miles to church and Sunday School when the lady who first brought me to church was unable to attend. As I grew up and no one in my family was actively involved in church I drifted away. I learned to play the guitar and wound up in a family band named "The Country Kings." It consisted of my wife' sister, her brother, a brother-in-law and his brother. We were good and once playing at a dance an individual came up to us and told my sister-in-law if we wanted to quit playing for "peanuts", call him and we could go big time. That never took place because of all things God used a Hank Williams 8 track Gospel cassette that I gave to a friend that started him to thinking about his relationship with God and wound up getting saved in an Independent Baptist Church. He then began immediately witnessing to me and everyone else to the point he was fired from his job as my Pipefitter helper. His constant witnessing paid off because I wound up joining a little Baptist Church near home and eventually started my own Gospel singing Group, "The Woodard Family Bluegrass Gospel singers and we still sing from time to time today after all these years.

Once a child of God is saved and indwelled by The Holy Spirit there is an awareness of sin in their life. For a child of God to "Live it up" carries consequences. Many will stand at the Judgment Seat Of Christ with no rewards to show for their life lived after salvation.

1 Corinthians 3:13-15
13 Every man's work shall be made manifest: for the day shall declare it, because it shall be revealed by fire; and the fire shall try every man's work of what sort it is.

14 If any man's work abide which he hath built thereupon, he shall receive a reward.
15 If any man's work shall be burned, he shall suffer loss: but he himself shall be saved; yet so as by fire.

Note in verse 13 that the basis of rewards given is not how many works one has but rather what sort or why one worked for the Lord. The motive for serving Jesus is to be done out of love for what He has done for us and continues to do everyday in keeping us safe and secure in God's family.

Hebrews 12:6-8
6 For whom the Lord loveth he chasteneth, and scourgeth every son whom he receiveth.
7 If ye endure chastening, God dealeth with you as with sons; for what son is he whom the father chasteneth not?
8 But if ye be without chastisement, whereof all are partakers, then are ye bastards, and not sons.

Below are some of the things that befalls a believer in this life who lives in open sin and rebellion against God.

1 Corinthians. 11:30 For this cause many are weak and sickly among you, and many sleep.

    a. Those who made a mockery of the Lord's Supper had two fates.

1. God struck some of them with sickness.
2. God killed some of them.

1 John 1:4 Ye are of God, little children, and have overcome them: because greater is he that is in you, than he that is in the world.

    A person living in sin has no joy and fellowship with God.

2 John 1:8 Look to yourselves, that we lose not those things which we have wrought, but that we receive a full reward.

    Things is plural, salvation is singular.
    The things that true believers can and sadly lose, is opportunities to serve God and be a part of winning people to Jesus.
    In closing:
    How does sin in the life of a believer affect His relationship with God?

    a. First of all sin cannot break the relationship from God's family, anymore than a child can be unborn from a family once they are born into it. No going back in time.

    b. The fellowship can be broken when sin enters a believer's life if he doesn't repent and turn from it.

    c. If a believer continues to live in sin after the Holy Spirit continues to convict him or her of it, God can choose to chastise that child of that sin. The purpose being the believer will repent and the fellowship restored.

d. If a believer deliberately turns from God and is no longer being used in God's work, God has and can call that child home.

Illustration:

A father has a son and warns him not to play in the mud and he catches him playing in it with his friends. The father cleans the child up and puts clean clothes on him and tells him to stay out of the mud.

The child goes out and gets in the mud again. The Father reminds his son that he doesn't want him in the mud. The child is sorry he has hurt his father and promises to not do it anymore.

The child goes back out and gets back in the mud, not caring about his father's warnings. The father sees his son and warns him, that if he doesn't get out of the mud, he will whip him.

The child continues to play in the mud, even talking his friends into getting into it with him. The father looks outside and sees what's happening and goes out and whips his son and tells him to stay out of the mud.

One hour later, the father looks outside and his son is back in the mud with his friends. The father says" Son, I warned you about getting dirty, I whipped you for getting dirty, you refused to mind. The father says "Son, come in the house, I know how to keep you out of the mud."

1 John 4:4 Ye are of God, little children, and have overcome them: because greater is he that is in you, than he that is in the world.

Chapter VII
Conclusion

As we conclude this brief study on eternal security I pray that you will understand that to believe in the eternal security of the believer can never in God's eyes be used to live in open rebellion against God and then die and go to Heaven and be greeted by Jesus with outstretched arms welcoming him or her home.

Matthew 25:23 His lord said unto him, Well done, good and faithful servant; thou hast been faithful over a few things, I will make thee ruler over many things: enter thou into the joy of thy lord.

Notice that Jesus said that only faithful servants will be greeted with the words "well done." There can be many different kinds of servants as to what is required of them. There is one thing all servants have in common and that is to be faithful. As there will be different degrees of punishment for the unsaved there will be different degrees of rewards for the saved.

If you do not believe in the eternal security there are some questions I want to ask to all who may not believe or understand the truths of eternal security for true believers.

Do you believe Satan would be able to use his evil tactics to cause one of God's children to be saved and then lost? The answer is yes without a shadow of doubt. Satan hates God and all of God's children. His philosophy is "I know I am going to spend eternity in Hell and I want to take as many people as I can to Hell with me."

Since Satan hates God and all of His children and the reason he doesn't take them to Hell with him is that he cannot because they are kept by the power of God.

If he could have robbed you of salvation and didn't and you made it to Heaven, you would have to give him credit for going there instead of the One who suffered, bled and died on a cruel cross for you.

"If saved always saved", not "Once saved always saved." sounds better to me.

Romans 5:1 Therefore being justified by faith, we have peace with God through our Lord Jesus Christ:

The only true peace we can have with God is through a personal relationship with Jesus Christ.

Dr. Johnny Woodard

Note: No portion of this book may be used for personal gain but it can be used to promote the truths of God's Word.

Other Books Available Online

www.ingramcontent.com/pod-product-compliance
Lightning Source LLC
LaVergne TN
LVHW011900060526
838200LV00054B/4444